and planets. In Europe, some claimed that the Jews who lived among th
Christian population were poisoning their wells, leading to mass killings
of Jewish communities in Germany and France. Some even thought that
poisonous air, known as '**miasma**', was spreading the disease.

Treatments

With no understanding of what was causing the disease, ideas for
treatments were equally far-fetched. Remedies included drinking vinegar,
avoiding moist food, bleeding, and taking medicine made out of anything
from crushed jewels to insects. Some believed that they could sweat out
the disease, so sat between two raging fires, or wrapped themselves in
furs to induce sweating.

Medicine in medieval Europe was very basic. Doctors would place a frog
on the buboes in an attempt to absorb the poison, or even a severed
pigeon head. Some doctors came to realise that bursting the buboes could
cause the illness to stop, and became increasingly skilled at doing this with
a small lance to allow the pus to seep out.

However, sufferers kept on dying. The countryside was littered with
corpses in the fields and on the roadside. Whole communities became
ghost towns almost overnight. The plague was particularly bad in large
towns and cities, where corpses were thrown into mass graves, often little
more than ditches with a thin layer of earth to cover the dead.

The Scots realised the English people were in distress, and invaded England
in 1350. However, the Scottish soldiers soon caught the plague themselves,
and when they retreated north of the border, they spread the plague to
Scotland. Not even the clergy or royal family were safe from the plague.
Three Archbishops of Canterbury died in quick succession, and King Edward
III's daughter died while travelling to meet her new husband in Spain.

Fact

A recently excavated
mass grave near the
Tower of London
revealed plague sufferers
buried five deep.

Flagellants

During the Black Death, a religious sect called '**flagellants**'
took to travelling England in procession, whipping
themselves in punishment for their sins. Their reasoning was
that if they punished themselves, God would not see the
need to punish them also with the plague. Needless to say,
their method was not successful.

Illustration showing a procession of flagellants

Check your understanding

1. What proportion of England's population was killed by the Black Death?
2. What were the symptoms of the bubonic plague?
3. What was the most common explanation for the Black Death?
4. How were dead bodies dealt with in towns and cities during the Black Death?
5. Why did flagellants think that whipping themselves would save them from the Black Death?

Unit 6: Late medieval England
The Peasants' Revolt

By 1351, the worst of the Black Death was over in England. In some historians' estimates, it had killed around two million people.

Having lost such a large proportion of the country's population, landowners found it increasingly difficult to find enough peasants to work their land. Peasants knew that their services were in high demand, and started moving from farm to farm asking for higher wages. Edward III tried to stop this in 1351 with the **Statute of Labourers**, which fixed peasant wages at the pre-Black Death levels. However, peasants and landowners alike paid little attention to the law.

Class conflict

Enterprising peasants with money to spare were able to buy up the land and empty houses belonging to plague victims for rock bottom prices. This new class of landowners became known as yeomen, meaning a peasant with up to 100 acres of farmland. **Yeoman** farmers threatened the feudal hierarchy, and the status of its traditional landlords. Some survivors of the plague also turned against the authority of the Catholic Church, which had been powerless to explain or prevent the Black Death.

Power was slowly moving to the people, and the nobles were not happy. In 1363, the **Sumptuary Laws** were passed, laying out in detail what different classes were allowed to wear. Gold cloth and purple silk was reserved for the royal family; lords could wear fur and precious stones; and knights could wear fur-trimmed cloaks. Peasants were banned from wearing anything except plain cloth costing less than 12 pence a length.

Wat Tyler's rebellion

Tensions between the lords and the people came to a head in 1381. At this time the 14-year-old king named Richard II was sat on the throne. He left much of the government of England to his uncle John of Gaunt, an unpopular nobleman with little concern for the common people.

To help pay for the Hundred Years War against France, John of Gaunt established the **Poll Tax**. This was a one off tax of 4p to be paid by all adults over the age of 14 (poll means head, so it was literally a tax 'per head' on the English people). As the same price was to be paid by all people, rich or poor, the Poll Tax was deeply unpopular among England's peasants.

Fifteenth century manuscript depicting the meeting of Wat Tyler and John Ball in 1381

Collins

Key Stage 3
Medieval Britain

Late medieval England

Robert Peal

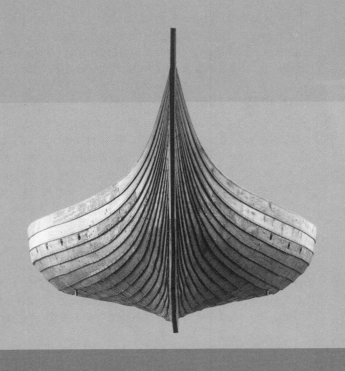

Knowing History

Unit 6: Late medieval England
The Black Death

During the 1340s, stories started to arrive in Europe of a dreadful disease ravaging the populations of far off lands in India and China. Such stories were common, but this one happened to be true.

The **Black Death** first hit European trading towns, such as Venice, in 1347. The first recorded deaths in England occurred in June 1348 at the port town of Melcombe Regis in Dorset. Within two years, this horrifying disease had killed between one third and half of England's population.

The pestilence

We now call this plague the 'Black Death', but people in medieval England would have called it the '**Pestilence**' or the 'Great Mortality'. The first symptoms were large swellings known as '**buboes**', which appeared in victims' armpits and between their legs and were said to resemble an onion.

The buboes then spread across the body, followed by blue or black blotches. Sufferers then started to vomit and spit blood, suffer from seizures, and their breath turned foul and stinking. After two to three days of horrific suffering, they would be dead. Occasionally, the buboes would burst, emitting a rancid smelling pus. However, this was a good sign, as it often meant the body was fighting back against the disease, and might overpower it. Named after the buboes, which were its first symptom, this variant of the disease is now known as the '**bubonic plague**'.

There was also a more lethal variant called the '**pneumonic plague**', which was spread through the breath. This version of the plague attacked the lungs, giving sufferers a fever, and leading them to choke to death with a bloody froth bubbling at the mouth.

Modern illustration of a town turning away visitors during the Black Death

Explanations for the plague

Today, we know that the bubonic plague was caused by bacteria, which was spread by fleas living on black rats. The rats would have lived on merchant ships, and run to shore across rigging ropes attaching a ship to the harbour. However, during the medieval period, people had no understanding of what was causing great swathes of their population to die.

The explanations that people did devise show the power of religion and superstition in the medieval mind. Most people believed the plague was punishment sent down by God, who had been angered by greed and sin on earth. Others believed that it was caused by an alignment of stars

On 30 May 1381, a royal official arrived in the Essex town of Brentwood to collect the new tax. The Essex peasants refused to pay, killing the official's clerks and sending him fleeing back to London. Within three days the whole county of Essex was in open rebellion against the king, and thousands of Essex peasants decided to march on London.

At the same time, a yeoman named Wat Tyler organised around 4000 peasants to march on London from the nearby county of Kent. Armed with bows, clubs and axes, the rebels reached London on 13 June. Here a radical preacher, John Ball, rallied them with a speech, in which he asked: "When Adam delved and Eve span, who was then the gentleman?"

Once inside London, the rebels stormed Newgate and Westminster prisons, and burned John of Gaunt's sumptuous **Savoy Palace** to the ground. One of the most unpopular figures in the King's government was the Archbishop of Canterbury, Simon Sudbury. The peasants executed him on Tower Hill alongside the Lord High Treasurer Sir Robert Hales, and their heads were placed on spikes and paraded around London.

Great Coxwell Barn, Oxfordshire. Medieval peasants were expected to pay tax to the Church and their landlord in 'tithe barns' such as this

Richard's response

To bring an end to this chaos, Richard II agreed to meet the rebels outside London at a place called Smithfield on Saturday 15 June 1381. Their leader, Wat Tyler, rode out to negotiate with Richard. Accounts vary as to what happened next. Some say Tyler attacked Richard's men, others that he rudely spat on the ground. Either way, a struggle ensued during which Tyler was run through with a sword and killed.

Richard seized the initiative, and promised to agree to the peasants' demands so long as they returned to their towns and villages. They duly did so, but the king had little intention of keeping his promise. Richard II went back on every concession he had made to the rebels, and 200 of their leaders were tracked down and hanged. The **Peasants' Revolt** may have been a failure, but feudal England had been challenged. Over the next two centuries, England's peasants gradually became freemen, and were no longer tied to working for their feudal lords.

Fact

The king's mother Princess Joan was known as the 'Fair Maid of Kent', and was famous for her beauty. When the rebels found her, one of them demanded she kiss him. Joan was said to have fainted in shock.

Check your understanding

1. How did the government respond to the growing wealth and power of medieval peasants?
2. Why was the Poll Tax so unpopular among medieval peasants?
3. What parts of England did the peasants who took place in the revolt come from?
4. What did the peasants do once they reached London?
5. How did Wat Tyler die?

Unit 6: Late medieval England
The Wars of the Roses

Crowned in 1423, Henry VI was England's youngest ever king at just nine months old. For the first 16 years of his life, a royal council governed England on his behalf.

When Henry VI came of age, he fell well short of the great expectations set by his father Henry V, the hero of Agincourt.

England had been steadily losing its French territories to a newly powerful French king, Charles VII. When England lost Normandy, the 18-year-old Henry VI was expected to fulfil his duty and lead the English army into war. Instead, he sent his cousin to do the job. Henry VI hated the idea of war, and was the first medieval king never to lead his army on the battlefield. He preferred books and churches to swords and armour. Many of Henry VI's noblemen believed their king was, quite simply, a coward.

By 1450, England's French empire was once again reduced to the small port town of Calais. That year, a rebellion broke out in London, with three days of open fighting in the streets led by a rebel named Jack Cade. The rebels dragged a former minister of the king from the Tower of London and beheaded him.

To make matters worse, in 1453 King Henry VI suffered the first of many bouts of madness. For a year he was completely unresponsive to anything around him, and the king had to be cared for like a new-born child.

Illustration depicting the Lancastrian King Henry VI

The Yorkist threat

Henry VI was clearly incapable of ruling, so power passed to a group of powerful noblemen. Chief among them was the King's cousin, a wealthy nobleman called Richard, Duke of York. Henry VI's French wife, Margaret of Anjou, however, despised the overly powerful Duke of York. Queen Margaret was a formidable leader, and she began to organise the opposition to the Duke of York.

This led to two rival factions forming in the mad king's court. The followers of the Duke of York, known as the 'House of York', were on one side. The supporters of the king led by Queen Margaret, known as the 'House of Lancaster', were on the other. Though they did not use them at the time, the two sides are today identified by two roses – a white rose for the **Yorkists**, and a red rose for the **Lancastrians**.

Symbol of the red Lancaster rose

Symbol of the white York rose

Outbreak of war

In 1459, Margaret declared the Duke of York a traitor, and war broke out between the House of York and the House of Lancaster. **The Wars of**

the Roses had begun. Queen Margaret took control of the Lancastrian forces, and quickly gained the upper hand, defeating the Duke of York at the battle of Wakefield in December 1460. The Duke was cornered on the battlefield by Lancastrian troops, and beheaded. Margaret ordered that his head should be placed on a spike outside the gates of the city of York, and adorned with a paper crown.

Queen Margaret's success did not last. The people of London refused to allow her into their city, and Margaret had to withdraw to the North of England. Meanwhile, with Richard the Duke of York now dead, his son Edward took on the leadership of the House of York. Aged only 18, he was everything that the mad King Henry VI was not. Standing 6 feet 4 inches, Edward of York was a proven warrior on the battlefield, and a charismatic leader.

In March 1461, he was crowned King Edward IV of England. To confirm his rule, Edward IV marched north to finish off the Lancastrians, and won a victory at the brutal Battle of Towton on 29 March. Henry VI and Queen Margaret fled into exile in Scotland and Edward IV secured his place as the first Yorkist King of England.

Fact

Henry VI was present at the Second Battle of St Albans in 1461, but the mad king spent the battle singing to himself while sitting under a tree.

Battle of Towton

Today it is largely forgotten, but the Battle of Towton is probably the single bloodiest battle ever fought on British soil. The Yorkist and the Lancastrian forces each numbered around 50 000 men, and they faced each other on a freezing cold morning in March.

Already brutalised by two years of fighting, ideas of chivalry had disappeared in England. An extreme level of bloodlust marked the battle. Skulls found at the site were covered with more than 20 wounds, suggesting that soldiers mutilated the dead bodies of their enemies. By the end of the day, 8000 Lancastrians lay dead, alongside 5000 Yorkists, and the snow-covered field was stained red with blood.

Modern illustration of the Battle of Towton

Check your understanding

1. In what way was Henry VI different from his father, Henry V?
2. Why did many nobles, such as the Duke of York, believe Henry VI was incapable of ruling England?
3. Who led the House of Lancaster at the beginning of the Wars of the Roses?
4. Who was crowned as the first Yorkist King of England in March 1461?
5. What can be learnt about the Battle of Towton from the skeletons that have been found on the site?

Yorkist rule

Aside from a short exile in France, Edward IV ruled England from 1461 to 1483. Overshadowed by the chaos of the wars that surrounded him, Edward IV is sometimes called England's 'forgotten king'.

As king, Edward was popular and charming, and brought a brief spell of prosperity to England. His power depended upon the support of his allies, and chief among them was the Earl of Warwick. Warwick groomed Edward to be king from an early age and was the true power behind the throne. One French visitor recalled at the time, "England has two kings, Warwick, and another whose name I have forgotten".

The Kingmaker

Edward IV wanted to break free from the control of Warwick. A romantic at heart, in 1464 he secretly married his true love, a commoner named Elizabeth Woodville. Such a marriage was unheard of for a king, who was expected to form a tactical alliance by marrying into another royal family. When the Earl of Warwick found out about Edward's marriage, he was furious.

In 1469, Warwick switched sides to the House of Lancaster. A year later he invaded England with Queen Margaret, who had been living in exile in France. Edward IV fled to Flanders and Warwick made Henry VI king once more, earning his nickname, '**The Kingmaker**'. However, Henry VI's second reign lasted for only a year. In 1471 at the Battle of Barnet, Edward IV defeated the Lancastrian army and the Earl of Warwick was killed. Henry VI died in prison, most likely murdered by Edward's soldiers.

For twelve more years, Edward IV ruled England in relative peace. However, in 1483 he caught a cold while fishing, and a few days later died aged just 40 years old.

The princes in the Tower

The death of Edward IV led to one last chapter in the Wars of the Roses. Edward IV had two young sons, aged 12 and 9, who were in Ludlow when their father died. The eldest, named Edward, was due to become King Edward V. His uncle, Richard the Duke of Gloucester, was chosen to rule as a **protector** on the young king's behalf.

Richard met the princes as they travelled from Ludlow to London, but when they arrived in the capital he imprisoned them in the Tower of London. Richard claimed it was for their own safety, but it soon turned out that the greatest threat to the princes' safety was Richard himself. Richard declared the marriage between his older brother Edward IV and Elizabeth Woodville invalid, ruling out Edward V's claim to the throne. He then had himself crowned King Richard III.

> **Fact**
>
> George Duke of Clarence was Edward IV's brother. He started the Wars of the Roses fighting for his brother but then betrayed him to fight for Henry VI and Warwick in 1469. George then switched back to Edward's side in 1471. Finally, George was killed for treason in 1478. He was allegedly drowned in a barrel of Malmsey wine.

King Richard III, uncle to the princes in the Tower

The Tower of London where the young princes were imprisoned

Richard III has long been remembered as the greatest villain of this period. In Shakespeare's play *Richard III* (written in 1592), he is depicted as an ugly hunchback with a withered arm, though how far this depiction is true is a source of debate. What is known is that once placed in the Tower, the princes were never seen again. In the years that followed a story emerged that Richard ordered the princes to be suffocated in their beds, smothered with pillows while they slept.

In 1674, labourers working at the Tower of London found a wooden chest hidden beneath a staircase containing two skeletons. They were of two children, one slightly older than the other. The skeletons were pronounced to belong to the two dead princes, and were reinterred at Westminster Abbey. In 1933, the tomb was reopened so that modern forensic methods could finally put the mystery to rest. Professor W. Wright concluded that, on examination of their teeth, the skeletons did belong to two boys, aged around eleven and thirteen. What is more, he believed a red mark on the facial bones indicated a bloodstain – something commonly caused by suffocation.

Modern illustration of the princes in the Tower of London

Back in the summer of 1483, rumours quickly started to spread across England that Richard III had killed the princes. Even in the savage context of the Wars of the Roses, killing your own brother's sons was a step too far. This perhaps explains why so few Englishmen rallied to Richard's cause when, two years later, war with the House of Lancaster resumed.

Check your understanding

1. What role did the Earl of Warwick play when Edward IV became king?
2. Why were Edward VI's subjects, in particular Warwick, so shocked by his marriage?
3. On what basis did Richard III make himself King of England in place of his nephew Edward V?
4. How did Shakespeare depict Richard III in his play, written a century after Richard's death?
5. What did the findings of Professor W. Wright appear to show in 1933?

The Battle of Bosworth Field

By the end of the Wars of the Roses, tracing the rightful claim to the throne in England's tangled royal family was no easy task.

In 1485, an unlikely new claimant to the throne emerged. Brought up in a windswept corner of south-west Wales, Henry Tudor's claim to the throne was tenuous. His Welsh grandfather was a servant to Henry V named Owain ap Maredudd ap Tewdwr. He miraculously married the widowed wife of Henry V in 1432, and anglicised his name to Owen Tudor.

Henry Tudor was a member of the House of Lancaster, and a man of great self-belief. He had spent the last 14 years of his life exiled in France, preparing his bid for the English throne. Henry was greatly helped by his formidable mother Margaret Beaufort. Margaret was the great-great-granddaughter of Edward III, and married Henry's father at the age of 12. And even that was her second marriage! At the age of 13 Margaret gave birth to Henry Tudor, by which time she was already a widow.

Henry Tudor's mother, Margaret Beaufort

Margaret went on to marry twice more. She was a skilful political operator, moving her support between the Houses of Lancaster and York when it suited her and her beloved son best, waiting for the best moment for Henry to strike.

On 1 August 1485, Henry Tudor landed on the coast of his homeland of Wales, and marched towards England. With a force of just 1000 mostly French soldiers, Henry hoped to gather troops along the way. However, the response of the war weary nation was not good. As Henry reached the English midlands for his showdown with King Richard III, his forces numbered just 5000 men.

Bosworth Field

Richard III set up camp on 21 August, securing the high ground at a location known as Bosworth Field. His Yorkist army numbered perhaps 10 000 men, and he also had the help of cannon fire, a recent technological advance in medieval warfare.

Modern illustration of the Battle of Bosworth Field

Outnumbered, and poorly positioned at the foot of the hill in a marshy bog, there was little reason to expect Henry Tudor's Lancastrian forces to win. Richard III led a Yorkist cavalry charge against the Lancastrian forces, but one of Henry's French **pikemen** knocked Richard III off his horse. According to Shakespeare's retelling of the battle, Richard cried out at this moment: "A horse! A horse! My kingdom for a horse!".

It was around this time that Lord Stanley, who was Margaret Beaufort's fourth husband, chose to tip the balance of the battle. Stanley had 3000 men, but had so far watched the battle unfold from the sidelines. As the battle started to turn against Richard, Lord Stanley sent in his soldiers to seal the victory for Henry.

All sources agreed that Richard III died heroically, fighting off his attackers until he was cornered, overpowered, and killed. According to legend, Lord Stanley found Richard III's gold crown in a thorn bush, fished it out, and placed it on Henry Tudor's head. Meanwhile, the dead King Richard III was stripped naked and slung on the back of a horse. He was buried in an unmarked grave at Greyfriars church in Leicester, only to be rediscovered some 500 years later (see box).

Tudor dynasty

After his victory at the Battle of Bosworth Field, Henry Tudor became King Henry VII of England. He ruled in close partnership with his mother Margaret Beaufort. Margaret helped to arrange for Henry VII to marry Elizabeth of York, the daughter of Edward IV, and elder sister to the murdered princes in the tower. This well-judged marriage united the Houses of York and Lancaster, finally ending their 30-year feud.

There were rebellions against the new king, but Henry VII saw off his enemies and secured a lasting peace for England. Henry VII's new royal **dynasty**, the **Tudors**, would lead England into a great period of change. For this reason, Henry VII's reign (which ended with his death in 1509) is commonly seen as marking the end of the medieval period in English history.

Fact

To symbolise his union of the two houses, Henry created the **Tudor Rose**: the white rose of York sitting within the red rose of Lancaster.

The king of the car park

To this day, Richard III has his sympathisers. They claim he was a decent and honest king, whose reputation was later smeared by Tudor writers such as William Shakespeare.

Such sympathisers were overjoyed when, in September 2012, archaeologists found what was believed to be Richard III's skeleton beneath a car park in Leicester. Half a century after his death in battle, Richard III was finally given a king's funeral and burial at Leicester Cathedral in March 2015.

Tented site of the dig for Richard III's body under a car park in Leicester

Check your understanding

1. What was Henry Tudor's claim to the throne?
2. Who helped Henry Tudor prepare his bid for the English throne?
3. What happened to Richard III during his cavalry charge against the Lancastrians?
4. What was sensible about Henry VII's decision to marry Elizabeth of York?
5. Who do sympathisers of Richard III believe is responsible for his bad reputation in English history?

Knowledge organiser

1348 The Black Death hits England

1381 The Peasants' Revolt

Key vocabulary

Black Death A plague that devastated medieval Europe in the fourteenth century

Buboes Onion shaped swellings that were usually the first symptom of the Black Death

Bubonic plague The most common variant of the plague, named after the swellings on victims' bodies

Dynasty A succession of powerful people from the same family

Flagellant Member of a religious sect who whipped themselves in punishment for their sins

Lancastrian A supporter of King Henry VI, or members of his family, during the Wars of the Roses

Miasma The theory that disease is caused by the spreading smell of a poisonous cloud of 'bad air'

Peasants' Revolt A major uprising across England that took place thirty years after the Black Death

Pestilence Another term for disease, and one of the Four Horsemen of the Apocalypse

Pikemen Soldiers who carried 12-foot-long, steel headed pikes, used to stop cavalry charges

Pneumonic plague An even more lethal variant of the plague, which attacks the lungs

Poll Tax A flat rate tax paid by all adults, literally meaning 'per head' of the English people

Protector A nobleman ruling on the behalf of a young monarch until they come of age

Savoy Palace John of Gaunt's sumptuous medieval home, destroyed during the Peasants' Revolt

Statute of Labourers A 1351 law which fixed the maximum wage for peasants at pre-Black Death levels

Sumptuary Laws Rules explaining what clothing different ranks within the feudal system could wear

The Kingmaker A nickname given to the Earl of Warwick during the Wars of the Roses

Tudor Rose A white rose of York sitting within the red rose of Lancaster, symbolising union

Tudors The royal dynasty that ruled England from 1485 to 1603

Wars of the Roses A series of wars between the houses of York and Lancaster lasting for thirty years

Yeomen A new class in late medieval England: commoners who farmed their own land

Yorkist A supporter of the Duke of York, and later his sons, during the Wars of the Roses

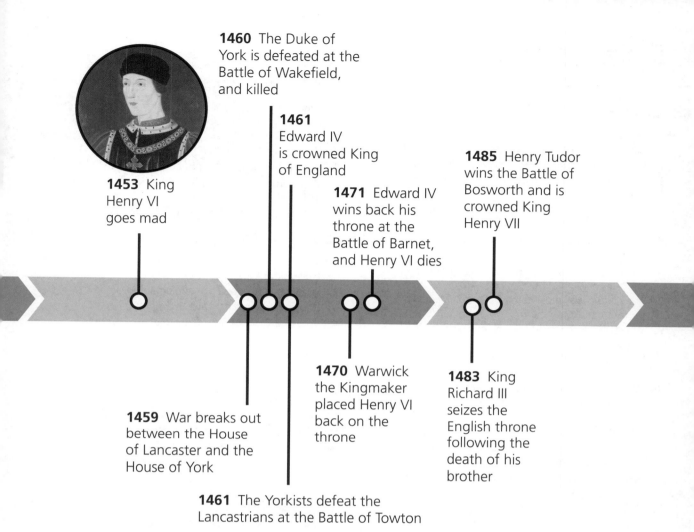

1453 King Henry VI goes mad

1460 The Duke of York is defeated at the Battle of Wakefield, and killed

1461 Edward IV is crowned King of England

1471 Edward IV wins back his throne at the Battle of Barnet, and Henry VI dies

1485 Henry Tudor wins the Battle of Bosworth and is crowned King Henry VII

1459 War breaks out between the House of Lancaster and the House of York

1461 The Yorkists defeat the Lancastrians at the Battle of Towton

1470 Warwick the Kingmaker placed Henry VI back on the throne

1483 King Richard III seizes the English throne following the death of his brother

Key people

Edward IV Son of the Duke of York, he was the first Yorkist King during the Wars of the Roses

Elizabeth of York The elder sister of the murdered princes in the tower, who married Henry Tudor

Elizabeth Woodville The wife of Edward IV, who controversially did not come from a noble family

Henry Tudor The last Lancastrian claimant to the throne, who started a new dynasty in 1485

Henry VI The mad Lancastrian King at the start of the Wars of the Roses

John of Gaunt The powerful uncle of Richard II who ruled on his behalf

Margaret Beaufort The mother of Henry VI, who played a central role in his bid for the throne

Margaret of Anjou The French wife of Henry VI, who took charge of the House of Lancaster

Richard III The youngest brother of Edward IV, who seized the English throne from his nephews

The Earl of Warwick A powerful nobleman who helped both Henry VI and Edward IV take the throne

Wat Tyler Leader of the Peasants' Revolt, thought to have been a yeoman from Kent

Quiz questions

Chapter 1: The Black Death

1. What proportion of England's population is thought to have died during the Black Death?
2. In what year did the Black Death arrive in England?
3. What swellings were usually the first symptom of the Black Death?
4. What variant of the plague was named after the swellings on victims' bodies?
5. What more lethal variant of the plague attacked the lungs of its victims?
6. The plague was probably spread by what insect, living on what animal?
7. The plague was most commonly explained as a punishment from whom?
8. What theory suggested the plague was caused by a spreading cloud of 'bad air'?
9. Which country invaded England in 1350, seeing that it was suffering from the plague?
10. What religious sect whipped themselves in punishment for their sins to avoid the plague?

Chapter 2: The Peasants' Revolt

1. What 1351 law attempted to fix the maximum wage for peasants at pre-Black Death levels?
2. What effect did the plague have on land and house prices in England?
3. What new class of commoners who farmed their own land arose in late medieval England?
4. What 1363 law established the clothing that different ranks in society could wear?
5. Which powerful nobleman ruled on behalf of his nephew, Richard II, at this time?
6. What flat rate tax paid by all adults helped to spark the Peasants' Revolt?
7. In what two counties did the Peasants' Revolt begin?
8. Who led the Peasants' Revolt?
9. What leading member of the church, named Simon Sudbury, did the peasants execute?
10. How many participants in the Peasants' Revolt did Richard II execute in retaliation?

Chapter 3: Wars of the Roses

1. Henry VI was the first medieval king not to do what?
2. What happened to Henry VI in 1453, which made him incapable of ruling his country?
3. Which nobleman ruled England on Henry VI's behalf?
4. Which side came to be represented by a red rose during the Wars of the Roses?
5. Which side came to be represented by a white rose during the Wars of the Roses?
6. Who led the supporters of King Henry VI during the early stages of the Wars of the Roses?
7. What setback occurred following the Queen's victory at Wakefield in December 1460?
8. Who was crowned King of England in 1461?
9. What brutal battle confirmed the new king's rule in 1461?
10. What record does the Battle of Towton hold?

Chapter 4: Yorkist rule

1. Which powerful nobleman secured support of Edward IV's reign?
2. What was this powerful nobleman's nickname?
3. Who did Edward IV marry in 1464?
4. Why was Edward IV's marriage controversial?
5. How did Edward IV die?
6. Who was next in line to the throne following the death of Edward IV?
7. Who seized the throne following the death of Edward IV?
8. Where were Edward IV's two sons imprisoned?
9. Who wrote a play about these events in 1592?
10. What was found in the building of the prince's imprisonment by labourers in 1674?

Chapter 5: The Battle of Bosworth Field

1. Who did Henry Tudor's grandfather, Owen Tudor, marry?
2. What 'House' did Henry Tudor belong to during the Wars of the Roses?
3. Who was Henry Tudor's mother?
4. Which English king was Henry Tudor's mother descended from?
5. In what year did Henry Tudor invade England to claim the throne?
6. Who knocked Richard III off his horse during his cavalry charge?
7. Who intervened to tip the balance of the battle in Henry Tudor's favour?
8. Who did Henry VII marry having become king?
9. What symbol was developed to represent the new ruling dynasty of England?
10. In which city was Richard III found buried beneath a car park in 2012?

William Collins' dream of knowledge for all began with the publication of his first book in 1819. A self-educated mill worker, he not only enriched millions of lives, but also founded a flourishing publishing house. Today, staying true to this spirit, Collins books are packed with inspiration, innovation and practical expertise. They place you at the centre of a world of possibility and give you exactly what you need to explore it.

Collins. Freedom to teach

Published by Collins
An imprint of HarperCollins*Publishers*
The News Building
1 London Bridge Street
London SE1 9GF

Publisher: Katie Sergeant
Editor: Hannah Dove
Author: Robert Peal
Fact-checker: Barbara Hibbert
Copy-editor: Sally Clifford
Image researcher: Alison Prior
Proof-reader: Ros and Chris Davies
Cover designer: Angela English
Cover image: robertharding/Alamy
Production controller: Rachel Weaver
Typesetter: QBS
Printed and bound by Martins, UK

Acknowledgments

Every effort has been made to trace copyright holders and to obtain their permission for the use of copyright material. The publishers will gladly receive any information enabling them to rectify any error or omission at the first opportunity.

The publishers would like to thank the following for permission to reproduce copyright material:

(t = top, b = bottom, c = centre, l = left, r = right)

Cover & p1 robertharding/Alamy; p2t Private Collection/© Look and Learn/Bridgeman Images; p2b Private Collection/© Look and Learn/Bridgeman Images; p3 Mary Evans Picture Library/Alamy; p4 Florilegius/Alamy; p5 Derek Croucher/Alamy; p6t Private Collection/Bridgeman Images; p6c Jane Rix/Shutterstock.com; p6b Jane Rix/Shutterstock.com; p7 Private Collection/© Look and Learn/Bridgeman Images; p8 Everett - Art/Shutterstock.com; p9t Salparadis/Shutterstock.com; p9b Private Collection/© Look and Learn/Bridgeman Images; p10t Georgios Kollidas/Alamy; p10b Lanmas/Alamy; p11t © Walker Art Gallery, National Museums Liverpool/Bridgeman Images; p11b David Warren/Alamy

Key Stage 3
Medieval Britain
Late medieval England

The Knowing History unit booklets help you to:

• Think critically about the past by focusing on the knowledge you need and then checking your understanding.

• Learn history through extraordinary people, amazing facts, and a distinctly engaging narrative.

• Remember key dates, vocabulary and significant people with the 'Knowledge organiser'.

• Test your knowledge with 'Quiz questions' for each chapter.

Knowing History Medieval Britain booklets

Anglo-Saxon England	978-0-00-819526-7
Norman England	978-0-00-819527-4
Medieval life	978-0-00-819528-1
Medieval kingship	978-0-00-819529-8
The Crusades	978-0-00-819530-4
Late medieval England	978-0-00-819531-1

The Medieval Britain booklets are also available in:
Medieval Britain 410–1509 Student Book 1

**Medieval Britain
410–1509
Student Book 1**
978-0-00-819523-6

**Early Modern Britain
1509–1760
Student Book 2**
978-0-00-819524-3

**Modern Britain
1760–1900
Student Book 3**
978-0-00-819525-0

Free Teacher Guides available on www.collins.co.uk

Collins
FREEDOM TO TEACH
Find us at **www.collins.co.uk**
and follow our blog – articles and
information by teachers for teachers.
🐦 @FreedomToTeach

ISBN 978-0-00-819531-1

9 780008 195311 >